AUSTRALIA'S
SYDNEY
A Celebration

AUSTRALIA'S

HELICOPTER PHOTOGRAPHY

SYDNEY *A CELEBRATION*

BY RON ISRAEL AND JOHN BARNAO   TEXT BY BRUCE ELDER

MURRAY DAVID

First published in 2000 by
Murray David Publishing Pty Ltd
Publishing Director: Murray Child
Marketing Director: David Jenkins
35 Borgnis Street, Davidson , New South Wales,
Australia, 2085

Consulting Publisher and Designer:
Sam Ure-Smith
Promotions Manager: Pam Seaborn
Edited by Merry Pearson

The publishers would particularly like to thank
the Sydney publisher, Caroline Simpson, for her
overall interest and involvement in this project.

ISBN 1 876411 71 6

© Photographs: Ron Israel and John Barnao, 2000
© Text: Bruce Elder, 2000
Electronically typset and composed
by the Publisher
Digital film by Typescan, Adelaide
Printed in Singapore

PAGE 1: *Whether it is Australia Day, New Year's Eve or any one of a dozen other special occasions, it is always time for a good fireworks display with the pyrotechnics filling the sky and being mirrored in the harbour waters. Here Sydney celebrates the New Year's Eve on 31 December, 1999.*

PAGES 2 AND 3: *This is the view awaiting those airline passengers lucky enough to arrive from the east and sweep across the city before turning and approaching Kingsford Smith Airport. Sydney Harbour has over 240 km of foreshore, and the sun shines on the harbour for an average of 342 days every year. Many of the city's population of 4 million people swim in the harbour and at the nearby ocean beaches all year round. In fact, there are over 100 beaches within reach of the city's population.*

PAGE 4: *Stretching to the south of the city, like a collection of pale new moons edged by the pink roofs of the city's southeastern suburbs, are some of the city's most popular beaches. Immediately below is gentle arc of the famous Bondi Beach, then tiny Tamarama and Bronte. Far to the south lie the waters of Botany Bay, with the Kingsford Smith runways jutting out into the bay.*

PAGE 5: *To the north of the harbour, lies the strand of beaches at Manly, the first of the city's northern beaches, followed by Curl Curl, Dee Why, Collaroy and Narrabeen. Still more beaches stretch all the way to Palm Beach, and beyond Broken Bay lies the Central Coast.*

PAGE 6: *The sails of the Opera House arc gracefully as though waiting to be caught by a brisk breeze. Above the harbour's dark waters, like a celebration in pointillism, a million multicoloured balloons float towards the heavens commemorating Coca-Cola's sponsorship of the 1996 Atlanta Olympic Games. This is Sydney at its most beautiful and celebratory.*

PAGE 7: *Dawn over the city. Honey-coloured early morning light catches the tops of the trees in Parramatta Park on Australia Day, and a spray of multicoloured hot air balloons, all gas and excitement, catch the gentle thermals. Before the day is out, the daring passengers in the cane baskets will have experienced the magnificence of Sydney from a vantage point once only enjoyed by the gods and creatures with the gift of flight.*

Afternoon sun plays on the water and on one of the many sailing craft on a typical day on Sydney Harbour.

Dedication

I dedicate this book to my late wife Leanora, who in 1942 first taught me how to load a Box Brownie.

Ron Israel

It is not every day that photographer Ron Israel and helicopter pilot John Barnao, while flying across the city, come across an upside down helicopter above the Opera House. The occasion: a new and special helicopter, the Aerospeciale Tigre made in France, was being put through its paces. The company was hoping to sell it to the Australian Defence Forces.

A note from Ron and John

The following are included in the definitions appearing in Australia's *Macquarie Dictionary*:

... celebrate ... to make known publicly; proclaim ... to sound the praises of; extol ... to engage in a festive activity; have a party.

Enjoy ...

By the way, we don't fly upside down!

Acknowledgements

My greatful thanks are due to the following:

Sam Ure-Smith and Murray Child for the time and effort they spent to make the book as you see it now; Mark Sotheran of *Agfa* for his help and enthusiasm; Kevin Cooper of *Fuji* for his technical advice and co-operation; Hans Chr. Brandt of C.R. Kennedy for his advice and help with the much admired Pentax 6 x 7 11 camera; and Simon Bates, whose flying skills and co-operation with the Jet Ranger were greatfully appreciated.

I would also like to thank Terry, Kym and the staff at Typescan, Adelaide who worked with the publishers and whose cheerful and careful attention to detail has produced such superb reproduction material.

Finally, my thanks go to John Barnao, a good pilot and friend. Without his understanding of aerial photography, my task would have been extremely difficult.

Ron Israel

PAGES 14 AND 15:

OPPOSITE: *The Anzac Bridge, which links the city to the west and to harbourside suburbs such as Balmain, has been beautifully lit at night since early 2000.*

OVERLEAF: *Built at Kincumber on the Central Coast just north of Sydney, the Stealth express cruiser carves a sharp curve in the blue waters in front of the Opera House. The appeal of the harbour, as the waterfront residents all know, is that it is constantly changing. One day a dramatic speedboat. The next a gracious liner, an express cruiser, a dirty coastal steamer or a tall ship.*

13

Introducing Sydney BRUCE ELDER

ARRIVING IN SYDNEY by air has been, for the vast majority of travellers, the culmination of a long and exhausting journey. Whether the travellers boarded the aeroplane in London, New York, Rome, Tokyo or Los Angeles, they are ready to get their tired legs back on terra firma and let their bodies, once again, experience a natural atmosphere.

For first-time visitors, there is a sense of high anticipation. At last they are about to touch down on 'the land down under', perhaps to make contact with friends or relatives they haven't seen for years. What will this great southern land be like?

Australians returning home will know what to expect. There will be the warm and friendly reunions at the airport. On a sunny day, there will be those blue skies, and that strong southern light which makes you squint, blink and wonder 'Was the northern hemisphere really as dull as this temporary blindness suggests?' In summer, there will be the inevitable trip to the beach to renew that universal Australian love affair with rolling waves, breakers and sun-kissed sands.

Planes from distant places always seem to arrive at Sydney's Kingsford Smith Airport in the early morning. The ritual is always the same. Wake up the passengers just before dawn for a quick breakfast on the plane. Passengers gaze out the tiny portholes and watch as the sky turns lighter and the arc of the Earth's curvature changes from dull grey to pink to a glorious slash of yellow-gold. Below, the blue-grey of the eucalypts which cover the Blue Mountains and the Great Dividing Range start to come into focus. If the plane is arriving from the East, the sea starts to dissolve from blue-black to blue. And then ...

Nothing can prepare the traveller for the heady magnificence of Sydney from the air. As the plane banks and prepares to line itself up the runway, the harbour city suddenly comes into view and there is an audible gasp from old and new passengers alike. This is not just another city. This is one of the wonders of the world.

ABOVE: *Hyde Park Barracks in Queens Square was built to the design of the famous convict architect Francis Greenway and completed in 1819. The barracks were constructed on the orders of Governor Macquarie to house convicts as they arrived in the colony. After transportation ceased in 1840, the building was used as accommodation for newly arrived immigrants. The barracks have been restored and are now used as a museum which features aspects of convict life in early New South Wales.*

OPPOSITE: *Adjoining the Royal Botanic Gardens are the grounds of Government House, this magnificent building which was home to New South Wales governors from 1845 until 1996. The incumbent governor now lives in his own home in a Sydney suburb. Government House is an impressive gothic revival style building overlooking the Harbour and the Opera House above Bennelong Point.*

Catch the harbour from the correct angle, with the morning sun reflecting off it and the Sydney Harbour Bridge and the Opera House silhouetted against the glorious silvery glare, and it will take your breath away.

Catch the city in the early morning light, with its red tile roofs glowing in the sun, and you'll see a city where a sprawling blue harbour is edged by endless washes of pink.

Catch the city during the day and you'll marvel at the bays, headlands and the tiny harbour beaches, or at the gracious curves of rocky outcrops and bushlands with coastal walking trails. This vast watery wonderland is edged by a necklace of fingernail-thin, new moon-shaped beaches which run all the way from Pittwater and Broken Bay in the north to Port Hacking in the South. It is extraordinary to realise that this city of bays, beaches and bushlands has no fewer than 111 beaches.

Sydney is a modern city. It is, in one sense, like any one of a thousand cities around the world. It has dramatic skyscrapers reaching to, and sometimes engulfed in, the clouds. The old central business district streets, constructed long before humans had even coined the term 'high rise', are now shadowy canyons where office workers gaze up to see the sun. Overpasses and underpasses gently curve around the CBD taking fast flowing traffic away from the city centre. Vast shopping complexes for the city's office workers take up entire city blocks and, through an elaborate combination of walkways and elevators, allow shoppers to walk for blocks without ever having to contend with road-level traffic.

But what makes the city special is the harbour, the water, the beaches. Always it is the water which can be as seductive and potent—if you surrender to its dark, sparkling beauty—as the canals and waterways of Venice. Sydney is unique— a city by the sea that is engulfed and seduced by its own watery magnificence.

The harbour has always kept visitors and travellers spellbound. But the visitor doesn't have to rely on Sydneysiders for glowing descriptions. Sir Arthur Conan Doyle, the creator of Sherlock Holmes, observed: 'The splendid landlocked bay with its numerous side estuaries and its narrow entrance is a grand playground for a sea-loving race. On a Saturday it is covered with every kind of craft, from canoe to hundred-tonner.'

And, in 1895, the American writer, Mark Twain, described the harbour as 'the darling of Sydney and the wonder of the world.'

Before there was a harbour, dinosaurs may have wandered the shores of a lake in the huge Sydney basin. When the whole area was uplifted, the Parramatta and other rivers scoured their courses through the steep mountain slopes that tumbled to the sea, creating a vast system of river valleys. Over time, the sea rose up and filled the

I9

deep V-shaped valleys with the blue-green waters of the Pacific Ocean. Where freshwater fish had once spawned in pools and fought against the rapids, whales wandered into the harbour and sharks came to the mangrove-infested upper reaches to breed.

Today, Greater Sydney city spreads for nearly 50 km from the CBD in all directions other than east. Historically, this gigantic bowl, which dips in the middle and rises to the north, south and west, has limited the growth of the city. Now, it has burst beyond this constraint and stretched into the scrubby bushland to the north of Broken Bay, up along the ridges of the Blue Mountains, and far out to the south-west along the Hume Highway.

The sandstone plateaux at the edge of the basin have poor sandy soil which sustains hardy native scrub—mostly stunted eucalypts, acacias and many varieties of resilient small bushes. This bushland is the home of poisonous spiders (the deadly Sydney funnelweb's natural habitat is the sandstone of the plateaux), snakes and lizards. To the south of the city, the Royal National Park, a vast stretch of bushland edged by peaceful beaches and rugged cliffs, gives a clear indication of how inhospitable such vegetation really is.

To the west of the city centre, in the vast postwar suburban areas which now stretch to the edge of the Blue Mountains, the soils are better. This is where the first farms were established and where, even today, market gardens still serve the city.

The first Aborigines came to this broad basin and harbour, probably around 40 000 years ago, but maybe much, much earlier. The local Aboriginal groups had no concept of migration. They did not have stories of how they had migrated across the Indonesian archipelago and, over thousands of years, slowly spread out across the island continent. To them, all things started in the dreaming, or the Dreamtime. That was their beginning and in their world, since the very beginning of time, they had always lived on the edges of this harbour. They had not arrived. They had always been here.

Life was good. Kangaroos and wallabies were abundant along the shoreline and in the bush. Smaller mammals—possums, echidnas, lizards, goannas—lived in the dead branches and trunks of the eucalypts which had fallen to the ground. The shores of the harbour were rich with food. At the time of European settlement, four distinct groups of Aborigines were living in the Sydney basin. From the northern shoreline of the harbour, stretching up the coast to what is now the Central Coast around Tuggerah, lived the Kuring-gai people. To the west of the modern CBD, and stretching across the Hawkesbury and Nepean Rivers and up into the Blue Mountains, lived the Dharug, who were described by the Eora peoples as the 'climbers of trees' and the 'men who lived by hunting'. To the south of the present city lived the Tharawal people. For six thousand years, since the ocean waters had flooded the bays and inlets, they had been fishing and collecting crustaceans and shellfish around Botany Bay and down the coast as far as Jervis Bay.

The group most directly affected by European settlement were the Eora people, the original Sydney residents, who lived around the foreshores of Sydney Harbour. The *Encyclopaedia of Aboriginal Australia* explains their lifestyle at the time of the arrival of Europeans as 'They were people of the harbour and the beaches. On a good day the harbour would be dotted with canoes (a fleet of 67 being counted in one day). Women fished from canoes with hook and line; men fished from the rocks with multi-pronged spears; lobsters were caught with small hoop nets; shellfish were prised from the rocks or dug from the sand and mud. Occasionally a whale came ashore and large groups of people came to feast. With such bounty the population was large and sedentary, with leisure to paint the walls of shelters and, on sandstone outcrops, slowly create the huge engravings which celebrated the sea.'

This was, by any conventional definition, an idyllic life. There were around 1500 people living around Sydney Harbour prior to European settlement. Today there are nearly 4 million. Those 1500 were living off food (lobsters, Balmain bugs, prawns, John Dory) which modern-day residents pay high prices for in the fish markets and the flashy fish

restaurants which dot the foreshores of the harbour. The produce was probably so rich that, on a good day, work was over by around ten or eleven in the morning. Then it was time to sit around the camp fire, gaze over the unspoiled beauty of the harbour, tell stories and gently fall asleep in the warm midday sun.

Into this antipodean Eden, on 26 January 1788, came a totally different world.

Eighteen years earlier, Captain James Cook, one of the most remarkable and gifted sailors and navigators the world has ever seen, sailed up the east coast of Australia. Cook entered Botany Bay and thought it suitable for a colony. He did not enter Sydney Harbour and, seeing it only from the ocean, did not recognise its unique deepwater facilities.

On 13 May 1787, a fleet of eleven vessels left Britain bound for Botany Bay toestablish a British port and penal colony in the South Pacific. The flagship of the fleet, the 520 ton HMS Sirius, was captained by Arthur Phillip who had been commissioned to become the colony's first governor. The vessels arrived at Botany Bay on the night of 19 January 1788.

Phillip quickly determined that Botany Bay, so strongly recommended by Cook for its good soils and deep grasses, was not suitable. On 21 January, accompanied by a detachment of marines, he rowed north in three small boats to explore Port Jackson and Broken Bay.

On the afternoon of 21 January, Phillip entered Port Jackson. He was later to write that it was 'one of the finest harbours in the world, in which a thousand sail of the line might ride in perfect security'. On that afternoon Phillip landed on the northern shore of the harbour, encountered about 20 unarmed Aborigines and, thinking them strong and friendly, named the beach they were standing on 'Manly'. The row boats then crossed the harbour and near the southern headland established a camp on a beach which, to this day, is called Camp Cove.

Phillip subsequently explored the southern shoreline, eventually finding a cove with deep mooring and a fresh stream which he named Sydney Cove, after Lord Sydney, who was the British Secretary of State at the time.

On 26 January, Phillip led the fleet north to Sydney Harbour. By the middle of the day, convicts were cutting down trees around the edge of Sydney Cove and, as the day came to an end, Phillip and his officers raised the Union Jack of Queen Anne and toasted the British royal family and the future of the colony.

The settlement started with nothing. Houses had to be built, streets and lanes carved out of the slopes on either side of the Tank Stream, quarters constructed for the soldiers and convicts, fields planted and the countryside explored. This was the true origin of Sydney. A desolate penal colony at the end of the world.

The first years in the colony were difficult. The supplies which had been brought

A prominent feature of Macquarie Street in Sydney is the Old Mint, which was once part of the Rum Hospital commissioned by Governor Macquarie in 1810. As a reward for their labours, the builders were granted the monopoly on rum imports into the colony. The construction of these and other new buildings during the administration of Governor Macquarie (1810–1821) gave Sydney town an air of unaccustomed dignity.

on the first fleet were inadequate. The tools were unsuitable and the expertise of both the convicts and the soldiers was limited. The colony patiently waited for ships to arrive from England, Batavia and the Cape of Good Hope. When none came, the colony was on the edge of starvation.

Conflict between Aborigines and Europeans occurred within months of the landing. As early as May 1788, a convict working beyond Sydney Cove killed an Aborigine, and shortly afterwards, two convicts were speared and killed while gathering rushes at the place now known as Rushcutters Bay.

By 1791, land had been granted to over 150 people in the hope that the agri-cultural base of the infant settlement could be broadened. Phillip pleaded with the British government to send out free settlers with farming experience so that the colony could become self-sufficient. By the mid-1790s farms, with convicts as labourers, were providing Sydney with supplies.

In the years that followed, a series of governors, most of them with military or naval backgrounds, battled to solve the problems of the new colony. The great challenge, however, lay inland from Sydney. The Blue Mountains seemed impassible to the explorers who made their way across the Sydney basin. When, after numerous attempts, they were finally crossed in 1813 by the explorers Blaxland, Wentworth and Lawson, the rush to settle the rich slopes to the west of the Great Dividing Range started in earnest.

It is appropriate that this major exploratory milestone was reached during the governorship of Lachlan Macquarie. Macquarie, who was governor from 1810 to 1821, transformed the struggling colony. During his administration, numerous public buildings were constructed with the help of the gifted architect and ex-convict Francis Greenway. Public education was introduced, the treatment of women and children was addressed, and the first bank (the Bank of New South Wales) was granted a charter.

The history of Sydney from 1825 until the 1860s is that of a colony slowly evolving into a society where free settlers and emancipated convicts worked together. The turning point occurred in May 1851, when Edward Hargraves brought 120 grams of gold to Sydney, triggering the goldrushes. Overnight, workers in Sydney downed tools and headed for the goldfields. Miners and prospectors from all over the world, eager to try their luck on the goldfields, passed through Sydney .

The city continued to expand throughout the 1870s and 1880s. At times its status as Australia's premier city was challenged by Melbourne, but it has remained Australia's major arrival point and the country's financial and industrial centre.

Somehow, even when Melbourne was awash with the gold from Bendigo and

The Holy Trinity, better known as the Garrison Church in the Rocks. Built between 1840 and 1878, the church sits in Argyle Place, Millers Point. It was the place of worship for the British garrisons stationed in Sydney in colonial times and to this day still serves the area as a church. It is open to visitors during the day.

city, ask only two questions: 'Would the Opera House look nearly as impressive if it wasn't edged by water?' and 'Why, when they are basically identical, is Sydney's harbour bridge known around the world and Newcastle-upon-Tyne's bridge barely known at all?' The answer is always 'The harbour. The harbour. The harbour.'

Today Sydney is a typical post-World War II modern city characterised by a high-rise central business district, elaborate and efficient urban transport and road links, and enormous suburban growth which means that the greater city is now similar in size to Los Angeles.

But a city is more than a collection of roads and buildings, of suburban sprawl and shopping malls. A city is a complex interaction between environment and inhabitants, and its texture creates the character of its inhabitants.

True Sydneysiders are a product of their environment. Over 200 years, the dour, grey discipline which characterised the convicts, the settlers and the surly overlords of those far off days has been slowly stripped away to reveal a group of people who are aggressively egalitarian, intolerant of pretension and artifice, gregarious to a fault, and sunny in a way that only people who live under constant blue skies can be.

There is an image of Sydneysiders which has become a kind of archetype for what the true Australian is really like. It is an image which, although it is deeply

Ballarat, Sydney has always been known as the 'premier city' in the 'premier state'. If it had been 'just another city', it may well have been overwhelmed by its rival, Melbourne. But it was not just another city. It was a city located on one of the most beautiful harbours in the world. No matter what it did, there would always be reflections off the waters. There would

always be the smell of salt and harsh sound of seagulls in the air. There would always be the steep slopes tumbling into the harbour. And there would always be the tens of thousands of people who wait patiently on the ferry wharves to glide to work across a sparkling harbour rather than get caught in a gridlocked traffic jam.

To understand the uniqueness of the

rooted in romantic notions of both the country and the city, has more than a passing element of truth. It sees Sydney as one never-ending holiday, with notions of 'sun, sand and surf' and 'bronzed Aussies'. The men are handsome and deeply tanned. The women are all gorgeous sun-bleached blondes. In this imaginary world, handsome men and beautiful women wake each morning, gaze out their window at the Pacific Ocean where the sub-tropical sun is sparkling off perfectly formed waves. They throw on casual clothes (shorts and T-shirts for the men), light, diaphanous frocks for the women, leap into sleek coupes and head for the beach for an early morning swim. The waters, of course, are warm and inviting. The beach is golden. After the swim they retreat to cafes and restaurants where crisp clean wines are served beside plates laden high with fresh seafood.

Sydneysiders, as they go off to another day at the office, know that this image in not true. But, like all romantic versions of the truth, they are unwilling to totally deny it. Sydneysiders may never have gone to Bondi Beach in great numbers on Christmas Day and New Year's Eve. When pale and pasty European tourists, in ever increasing numbers, flock to Bondi on those holidays, no one tells them that what they are doing isn't really very Australian. No one is going to dissuade them from thinking that Sydneysiders spend Christmas at the beach and that Australia is a country free from care and day-to-day worries.

It is true that Sydneysiders love their beaches. Most residents will make their way to their beach of choice during the summer months. They barely glance at the distinctive red and gold caps worn by the surf lifesavers whose dedication to

safety is admirable and selfless. They will, particularly if they are male, gaze in admiration at the glamorous young women lying topless or in the briefest of bikinis waiting for the summer sun to turn them golden brown. They will glance with tender amusement at the families gathered under the trees (so many Sydney beaches are edged by fine stands of Norfolk Island pines) for picnics and barbecues. They will watch the children building sand castles, consuming ice creams and playing beside the warm waters. And, somewhere deep inside they will admit that this really is paradise and say to themselves 'We really do live in the greatest city on Earth'.

In the minds of many people, particularly those from Europe, sunshine equals holidays and relaxation. In the minds of Sydneysiders it means outdoor activities.

Sydney is an intensely outdoors society. The average suburban home will have

some sort of barbecue facility out the back, and many homes also boast a private swimming pool. Rather than status symbols or benchmarks of success, these are natural additions to a lifestyle where casual clothes are worn most of the time, where watching or playing sport on the weekend is almost universal, and where, on any Sunday, tens of thousands of cars stream out of the suburbs heading for the coast.

It is always a challenge to define the qualities of people living in a particular city. Who is a typical Sydneysider? How is their life affected by where they live? Is it the well-dressed business executive walking briskly to an important meeting along the city streets? Or is it the truck driver or the labourer in their blue singlet and shorts letting the sun burn them an ever-deeper brown? Or is it the assistant serving in a sandwich shop or a department store and dreaming of the weekend when they will escape to the beach? The average Sydneysider is all of these people. In a city of four million people, no one occupation sums up the city's essence.

But there are characteristics which seem to belong uniquely to Sydney as a major Australian city. There is a sense of independence, a genuine sense of egalitarianism, a dislike of pretentiousness and a sense of energy and exuberance.

Somewhere deep in the past, possibly the convict past, lies a dislike of anyone in authority. Still, as many European visitors note with some amusement, Sydneysiders as a group are very law-abiding citizens. Somewhere deep in the city's psyche is the idea that if a government agency tells you to use a protective sun screen before you go out in the sun, then you do it. Equally, Sydneysiders are hugely proud of their surf lifesaving movement of public-minded people protecting foolish people who swim where they shouldn't swim.

Most Sydneysiders are unforgiving when it comes to social elites and aristocracies. They are proud of the fact that a person can become successful and can enjoy the city's riches. Some of the city's most beautiful waterfront houses are owned by people who started life with nothing and who, through hard work and enterprise, built a personal fortune.

Those who don't acquire 'airs and graces' with the money they made, are 'good blokes' (or women) and will be treated with good will and admiration. But, for those who believe they are 'better' or 'more important' than their less successful neighbours, the famous Australian 'tall poppy' syndrome comes into play. (Australians love to cut down to size anything that grows too big and fancies itself as being a little better and more beautiful than the rest of the flowers in the field.)

The history of modern day Sydney is full of stories of poor people, particularly immigrants from Eastern Europe after World War II, who stepped off refugee boats penniless and ended up as multi-millionaires. It is equally the story of

locals who have managed to create a fortune by doing everything from running a chain of liquor outlets to importing goods from Europe or Asia. These people, if they choose to, can clamber up the country's rather fragile social ladder by simply declaring their intentions.

To understand the true nature of Sydney, it is necessary to recall just exactly what was happening in Europe when the first non-Aborigines arrived on the shores of the great harbour. By 1788, the Industrial Revolution had started in Britain. Vast numbers of farm workers and peasants were moving to the industrial cities of Manchester, Birmingham, Liverpool and London looking for work. A new world—the world we still live in today—was about to overwhelm an old world of simple village life and people who worked long hours tilling the soil, sowing crops and tending farm animals. This new world, for better or worse, would see people working in factories, living in cities, replacing horses with motor cars, travelling from one country to the next with relative ease.

Sydney is essentially a post-Industrial Revolution society. There was never a time for a peasant class to establish themselves in Sydney and provide the city with a distinctive cuisine and a unique lifestyle. From its very beginning, it was a truly modern society where peasant foods, a regional style of housing, a regional language with a distinctly 'Sydney' accent simply did not have time to develop.

If you think of the great cities of Europe — Rome, Paris, London—each has its own special qualities, its own unique culture. In London, the accents are so distinct that South Londoners speak quite differently from East Enders and North Londoners.

Sydney arrived too late for that sort of unique culture to develop and so it has taken a little bit of every culture that comes its way. It is the true modern city— a hybrid city—where, if something is worth borrowing, then Sydney will embrace it and call it its own.

So when the great migration of Italians occurred in the 1950s, Sydney, at the time a very Anglo-Saxon city in the antipodes, saw the Italian coffee shop and liked what it saw. Today many inner-city Sydneysiders will start the day with a brisk walk down to their local cafe where they will order a latte, macchiato, espresso or cappuccino. They will probably accompany the coffee with a croissant or a Danish pastry. Some Australian diehards will demand raisin toast or toast and vegemite, while people yearning for Britain will order a full British breakfast with eggs, bacon and tomatoes.

Today's Sydneysiders are a bewildering mixture of cultural forces. They watch American movies at the local cinema, shop in large modern shopping malls, drive cars manufactured all over the world, watch television which is predominantly from America and Britain, listen to

OPPOSITE: *The old and the new are successfully combined in The Rocks. With its graceful curves, the Hyatt Hotel mixes it with carefully restored old buildings. At the shoreline at the left of the picture can be seen some of the superb restaurants on the waterfront housed in the old Campbells Storehouse. Numbers of old bond stores, so necessary to the activities of the nineteenth century Sydney port, tend to dominate the scene in this part of the well preserved historic area.*

the same pop music as the rest of the English-speaking world, read the same international bestsellers and, because of the enormous style power of the global village, basically look like the rest of the world. They may have their own special place in the sun, but they also want to be part of the larger world.

Sydney, Australia, in the twentieth century has slowly evolved from an unconfident British penal colony which then became a conventional colony still very much tied to Mother England's apron strings. Australia is now trying to assert its independence and become a confident nation that is actively involved in developing and prospering in its own region while trying to establish itself in the broader international community.

The city's history has been the nation's history. It has been a painful and often complex journey involving a search for some kind of defined national identity, an inordinate pride in physical attributes (both in war and on the sporting field), and a need to break from the narrow cultural values established by a predominantly Anglo-Saxon society.

With this in mind, the last decade has been a period of great change, with people of good faith trying to establish some pattern of reconciliation with Aborigines, with the vexing question of 'Who are we —these Europeans living on the southern edge of Asia?' being constantly addressed, and with the constant pressures of a truly multicultural and diverse society (which was once a virtual Anglo-Irish monoculture) bubbling to the surface and asking for resolution.

The old image of Sydney as a strange, predominantly Anglo-Saxon outpost of the British Empire is redundant. Even the 1960s–1970s image of an Anglo-Saxon with an overlay of non-English speaking southern and central Europeans is no longer relevant. The city has become multicultural and multinational. Inevitably, there has been racial friction, but it has, by the standards of other countries with large immigration programs, been low-level and rarely seriously violent.

The Sydneysider of the future will be distanced from any notion of England as 'home'. They will acknowledge that the Europeanisation of Australia was a result of British colonial expansionism in the late eighteenth century and will admit that there was once a society which looked to Britain for its political and legal institutions. They will rejoice in the sense that modern Sydney is a melting pot of cultures where people enjoy the benefits of older cultures while not being tied to the superiority of those cultures. The only thing that will slow these changes down is that Sydneysiders are basically easy-going. There are very few things that get them upset. It is not that they don't care, it is just that ... well, if you were living near a beach and basking under a sunny sky, would you feel the need to change anything?

RIGHT: *Photographed from the east of the city looking west, this view shows the Central Business District, Hyde Park, Macquarie Street, The Domain, the Art Gallery of New South Wales, Circular Quay and Darling Harbour.*

BELOW: *The entrance to the Art Gallery of New South Wales in Art Gallery Road.*

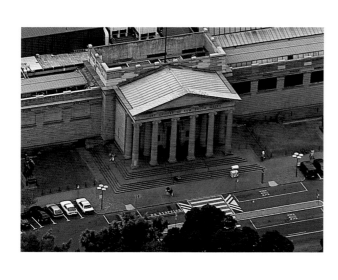

Sydney is the essence of Australia. It is essentially suburban, democratic, tolerant and easy-going. It is more interested in sport than intellectual activities; admires television and film stars more than politicians; and would always prefer to be having a few beers around the barbecue rather than sitting down in a dinner suit to a haute cuisine meal.

In this sense it is a true Mediterranean city in the Antipodes. A city of mild temperatures, of evenly distributed rainfall with slight maximums in the late autumn and early winter, and glorious, balmy subtropical summer days of sunshine, soaring temperatures, and people sunning themselves on the necklace of beaches which spread to the north and the south of the heads of Sydney Harbour. It is, after all, a city where the sun shines for an average of 342 days every year.

ABOVE: *To celebrate the Sydney 2000 Olympics and Paralympics, a series of sculptures of athletes were designed and lifted to adorn the edge of the city's highest building. The result is that residents and visitors can look heavenward from any vantage point in the city centre and see on the AMP Tower the sculptured symbols representing the city's commitment to athletes and their* quest for Olympic comradeship and success.

OPPOSITE: *Looking north from the AMP Tower with the magical assistance of a fisheye lens, there is a overwhelming feeling that this is a city surrounded by water, while the high-rise office blocks of the central business district reach for the heavens.*

OPPOSITE: *No matter where you are in Sydney's central business district you are never more than five minutes away from the harbour. Here, at Darling Harbour, where Market Street tumbles down from the city's heart, the old wharves have been turned into chic boulevards with cafes, restaurants and gift shops. And here, where once the clippers and tramp steamers unloaded goods from all over the world, gleaming new yachts and cruisers display their luxury at the Darling Harbour Boat Show.*

RIGHT: *Cities are dynamic. They change to meet the changing requirements of their ever-growing populations. For over a century, fruit and vegetables from around the country were bought and sold at Paddy's Markets. On weekends, it became a general market. There was always a sense of pulsating life about the building. But the city changed, and gardeners and merchants were fighting to get into the city centre, so the city's produce markets were moved to a location near the present Olympics site. The old market buildings are still used as an inner-city marketplace, and a multistorey building has been constructed above the old site.*

Each year on Anzac Day, 25 April, Australian soldiers gather to remember the battles they fought and their comrades and mates who died in action. In recent times, Anzac Day has attracted large crowds as Australians recall those who gave their lives for their country. In Sydney at dawn on Anzac Day, people gather around the Cenotaph in Martin Place to recall the dead. This is the official start of a day of memory and commemoration. These photographs were taken at the 2000 March when, despite heavy rain, marchers and onlookers turned out in large numbers.

LEFT: *Looking down on George Street, where the New South Wales State Governor takes the salute at the Sydney Town Hall. Part of St Andrew's Cathedral is seen in the lower left.*

OPPOSITE: *After passing the Town Hall, the marchers wheel left into Bathurst Street towards the end of the route.*

LEFT: *At the southern end of Hyde Park stands the Anzac Memorial. The memorial was designed by Bruce Dellit and the sculptures were made by Rayner Hoff. An art deco construction, it rises 30 metres above the Pool of Remembrance. Tenders for construction of the memorial building were called for in 1931 and it was officially opened by the Duke of Gloucester on 24 November, 1934. Inside, in honour of the soldiers who went to war for their country, is a Hall of Memory and a Hall of Silence. There is also an exhibition of photographs of Australians at War in the exhibition space underneath the building.*

OPPOSITE: *The expatriate Australian writer and journalist Clive James once described Sydney Harbour on a sunny day as looking like 'crushed diamond water'. On a clear sunny day, this is the perfect description for the eye-squinting magnificence which sparkles and gleams. The dark blue waters turn white and the harbour's two great symbols—the bridge and the Opera House—look like cardboard cutouts against the gloriously harsh antipodean sunlight.*

The old and the new. A replica of HMS Bounty, the vessel on which the famous mutiny took place in protest against conditions suffered by the crew when under the command of Captain William Bligh, passes the huge modern sails of the Opera House. Behind the Opera House stands Government House in its beautiful setting adjacent to Sydney's Royal Botanic Gardens.

OVERLEAF: In this picture, USS Constellation, a United States' aircraft carrier visiting the city in November 1999 is moored at the main wharf of Sydney's naval base at Garden Island, to the east of the city centre. The island was joined to the mainland in 1941 during the second world war, when, after the fall of Singapore the British needed a safe graving dock in the Pacific to serve allied fleets. The Captain Cook graving dock itself forms the peninsula joining the former island to the mainland.

Sydney Olympic Park at Homebush Bay comprises a number of separate venues.

LEFT: *The Tennis Centre.*

RIGHT: *The centrepiece is the Olympic Stadium, known as Stadium Australia, which cost $690 million. It will provide seating for 110,000 spectators during the games and 80,000 after the games. It is the largest Olympic stadium ever built..*

Sydney's Olympic Park is located at Homebush Bay, 14 km west of the city. It is situated on a 760 hectare site beside the Parramatta River, which is part of the upper reaches of Sydney Harbour. Part of the Sydney Olympics site is the 450 hectare Millennium Parklands, a conservation area beside the Parramatta River with more than 40 km of cycleways and pathways through a variety of landscapes that include river mangroves and undulating parks. This photograph, taken from 11 000 feet, shows the scene from the completed Olympic Park all the way across the city to the coast. Manly can be seen at the top far left and the runways of Sydney Airport stand out clearly in Botany Bay on the far right.

Sydney was awarded the 2000 Olympics in Monte Carlo on 23 September 1993. The main Olympic complex has been constructed at Homebush Bay. All athletes will live in one village on the site, and all other venues are within 30 minutes of the central site. 10 200 athletes will visit the city during this time and it is expected that the games will be watched by 3.5 billion people around the world.

1. *Stadium Australia*
2. *Sydney Super Dome*
3. *Sydney International Athletic Centre*
4. *Sydney International Aquatic Centre*
5. *Homebush Bay Novatel Hotel*
6. *Plaza Pylons*
7. *State Sports Centre*
8. *State Hockey Centre*
9. *New South Wales Tennis Centre*
10. *Olympic Park Railway Station*
11. *Sydney Showgrounds Exhibition Halls*
12. *Sydney Showgrounds*
13. *Sydney Showgrounds Showring/Baseball*
14. *Sydney Showgrounds Animals Pavillion*
15. *Millennium Parklands*
16. *Sydney Interanational Archery Park*
17. *The Brickpit*
18. *Bicentennial Park*

For a year prior to the Olympic Games, organisers held special events at Stadium Australia, with the aim to ensure that the Games would run smoothly. The state's major football codes—rugby league, rugby union and soccer—were all given nights for special events. When the rugby league held their special night, which attracted a capacity crowd to the stadium, it looked like this from the air.

OVERLEAF: Each Easter the country comes to the city. Farmers, graziers and livestock breeders bring their prize produce and livestock to the city to exhibit them at the Royal Agricultural Society's Easter Show. The highlight of the extended event is always the Grand Parade, in which the rural wealth of the state is on display. It is a reminder to the city that the produce of the country is vital for the well-being of the economy.

The Sydney Football Stadium, situated near Fox Studios and alongside the Sydney Cricket Ground at Moore Park, will be the venue for some of the Olympic events.

LEFT: *The White City in Sydney's eastern suburbs was the centre for lawn tennis throughout the majority of the twentieth century. Fans will remember the games played here by stars such as Hoad and Rosewell, Sedgman and McGregor. Newcombe and Laver. White City is still in use for local competition and its grand history is an inspiration for aspiring tennis players of the present. The new Tennis Centre at Sydney Olympic Park replaces White City as the major tennis venue and will no doubt be the scene for many exciting tennis events of the future.*

OPPOSITE: *Sydney is like a gigantic saucer that rises to the south, north and west from the wide, flat centre, which is dissected by the harbour. Looking towards the city centre from the west— just beyond the Stadium Australia at the Olympics site, it is easy to appreciate this simple geological design. Even taking into account the distortion created by a telephoto lens, this picture shows that Sydney certainly has the advantage of having its Olympic Park within easy reach of the central business district.*

Royal Sydney Golf Course occupies most of the green area between Old South Head and O'Sullivan Roads, Rose Bay, and is one of Sydney's most prestigious golf clubs. The lower right portion of the green area is Woollahra Golf Club, with Cranbrook School and Woollahra playing fields between the two courses. In this photograph, the area's close proximity to Bondi and Bondi Beach can truly be appreciated. The green area between New South Head Road and the harbour is home to Sydney Harbour Seaplanes, Rose Bay Ferry Wharf and Woollahra Wharf Sailing Club, and is the former home of the Rose Bay Flying Boat base so popular with wealthy travellers in the 1930s and 1940s.

LEFT: *Located only 8 km from the city centre and once known as Little Coogee, this narrow and attractive beach is protected from the full force of the Pacific Ocean by two rock platforms. It was named Clovelly after a local property which was owned by Sir John Robertson. Today, Clovelly is one of the best kept secrets among Sydney's southern beaches.*

OPPOSITE: *Nestled just to the south of Bondi and protected on both sides by the rugged cliffs which characterise the headlands south of Sydney, is the tiny surfing beach of Tamarama. Today, the foreshores are notable for the red tile roofs of the apartment blocks where residents enjoy spectacular views across the beach to the Pacific Ocean.*

RIGHT: *Sydney's famous Bondi Beach probably gets its name from the Aboriginal word* boondi, *which means the sound of waves breaking on a beach. It is a symbol of the city's beach culture, a constantly changing and evolving seaside destination where cafes and chic coffee lounges have replaced the grand old hotels and guest houses which once edged the main boulevard, Campbell Parade.*

OVERLEAF: *Edged by the warm waters of the Pacific Ocean and with the city centre only 8km away, the charming southern beach of Bronte has been a popular summertime seaside destination for Sydneysiders since the first Europeans settled there in 1842.*

PREVIOUS PAGES: *The huge red-roofed Coogee Bay Hotel fronts the beach, ensuring that the night life and the social life at Coogee are just as inviting as the beach life. In recent times, Coogee has become one of the most desirable beach residential areas in Sydney's southern suburbs, with many celebrities and personalities finding it quieter and more relaxed than nearby Bondi.*

ABOVE: *Offshore rowers from Coogee Surf Life Saving Club cut through the waters. The life saving movement, which started on Sydney beaches in 1906, is voluntary and dedicated to the protection and well-being of all members of the public who want to enjoy a swim or a surf on Sydney's magnificent ocean beaches.*

OPPOSITE: *One of the longest strands of beaches in Sydney lies where the shores of Botany Bay look out to the ocean. Here at Brighton-Le-Sands, a little south of Sydney Airport, can be found the tranquility of harbour bathing, provided that the bathing is always done within sharkproof nets such as the one pictured.*

LEFT: *Bare Island at La Perouse, named by Captain Cook in 1770, is now an historic site. The fort and gun emplacements were built in 1885 to guard Sydney's southern boundaries from possible attack.*

OPPOSITE: *The New South Wales Golf Course at La Perouse overlooks the entrance to Botany Bay discovered by Captain James Cook in 1770 on his voyage of discovery. The Golf Clubhouse can be seen in the centre of the picture, with Little Congwong Beach in the bottom right. The headland at the top right is Cape Banks.*

OVERLEAF: *Waves which have travelled thousands of kilometres across the Pacific Ocean break on Maroubra's golden sands during a surf carnival. On the beach, life-savers still keep a watchful eye as surfers frolic and dive in the clear waters of this popular southern Sydney beach.*

PAGES 78 AND 79: *North and South Cronulla Beaches, two very popular southern Sydney beaches. The Kingsway, Cronulla's main street,can be seen in the middle foreground with Gunnamatta Bay in the background.*

PAGES 80 AND 81: *The full beauty of the southern end of Sydney can be seen in this view taken over Port Hacking, with the little township of Bundeena immediately below. Burraneer and Cronulla can be seen in the middle distance, Caringbah to the left and Botany Bay in the distance.*

PREVIOUS PAGES: *Only a few kilometres off the Sydney Heads, the USS* New Jersey, *showed off its firepower on a training exercise during Australia's Bicentennial celebrations in 1988. If you look closely, you can see the projectiles which have been blasted from the huge guns.*

LEFT: *One of Sydney's most memorable annual events is the Sydney Harbour Ferry Race in which ferries of all sizes compete with each other in a race up the harbour. Given the unequal nature of the challenge (some ferries are just very much faster than others), it is more a fun activity than a serious race, with the smaller vessels all eagerly hanging around on the edges egging their favourites on to victory.*

ABOVE: *A tall ship cuts its way down the harbour. On occasions like this, a flotilla of smaller vessels—cruisers, catamarans, small sailing craft and even the Manly ferry—eagerly join the journey down the harbour and, with high spirits and a true sense of bon voyage, wish the ship farewell as it slips out the Heads.*

RIGHT *It is said that the best view of Sydney Harbour (for those not lucky enough to see it from the air) is the view looing south-west from Fairfax Lookout on North Head, south of Manly. This aerial view taken from above Manly Beach looking to the city confirms that, for sheer grandeur, there are few views to compare with this extraordinary vista.*

BELOW: *Shelley Beach at Manly boasts very expensive homes and apartment buildings, some with Harbour views, some with ocean views and some with both.*

LEFT: *Two hangliders soar on the updrafts around the cliffs at Warriewood, another popular northern beach.*

OPPOSITE: *One of the most popular surfing beaches of the north side is Freshwater Beach near Harbord. In the top of the picture is neighbouring Queenscliff Beach, which shares the strand with Manly's two beaches, North and South Steyne.*

LEFT: *The sweeping view from Dee Why to Long Reef. Dee Why Beach is a charming retreat with a huge variety of restaurants spread along the street fronting the beach, all with* al fresco *dining areas. The magnificent beach has plenty of room and grassy areas for great summer picnics. The walk along the beach to Long Reef headland is one of the best in the world, and nothing can match the glorious feel of a stiff sea breeze in the hair as the gentle climb over the skillion reveals more breathtaking views north to the central coast.*

OPPOSITE: *A striking view from North Curl Curl headland south over Curl Curl Beach and on to the city.*

OPPOSITE: *Collaroy Beach with its popular rock-pool in the foreground.*

RIGHT: *Mona Vale Beach looking south over Narrabeen Lakes to the city. First time visitors to the northern beaches area are always impressed by the variety and beauty of the string of beaches stretching from Manly to Palm Beach, a distance of around 25 kilometres.*

OVERLEAF: *A wonderland of water dotted with pleasure craft and marinas stretches north from Newport. Broken Bay and Lion Island stand guard over a stretch of water which reaches back into the Hawkesbury–Nepean river system. The unspoilt bushland of Ku-ring-gai National Park and Scotland Island edges Pittwater and beyond, the Central Coast blurs into a bewildering array of coves, beaches and rocky headlands. On the extreme middle right of the photograph the beaches of Newport, Bilgola and Avalon can be seen.*

93

There will always be an argument about the city's beaches. Does the north have better beaches than the south? Does it really matter, when the beaches stretch in a series of delicate golden arcs in both directions, and the residents flock to both to swim and surf. Here, Barrenjoey Road meanders past Newport Beach and sweeps around to begin the well-known 'Newport Bends', which take the motorist past Bilgola and on to Avalon and Palm Beach.

OPPOSITE: *Avalon Beach, the gateway to Clareville, one of the north's prestigious areas.*

RIGHT: *Whale Beach, Palm Beach and Barrenjoey. These exclusive areas are popular as permamnent homes or as holiday retreats.*

LEFT: *Looking at the the entrance to Pittwater from just over Palm Peach provides an astonishing view over Palm beach Golf Course, the northern reaches of Palm Beach and the Barrenjoey Headland, with the lighthouse perched in the middle distance. To the north is the Central Coast.*

A short boat journey from Palm Beach jetty on the Pittwater side brings one to the ever popular boating destination of The Basin. Providing fresh water and lots of recreation space, the little bay is an ideal retreat from the rigours of city life and can only be reached by water.

During April 2000, Harold Halvorsen the founder of Halvorsen Hire Cruisers, had his 90th birthday celebration. As a salute to the founder, the entire Halvorsen fleet moored at the company's marina while the celebrations took place at Coal and Candle Creek, a bay off the Hawksbury River near Pittwater. It would be a rare sight, indeed, to see the fleet altogether on any other occasion.

LEFT: *The wind's caught the sail. Quick, everyone onto the leeward side of the boat. Dangle your feet into the water and hope the weight of four people will be enough to keep the vessel steady and racing with the wind. This is what many people consider to be a perfect day on Sydney Harbour ... and a perfect way to spend that perfect day. Pictured is the former Sydney-Hobart contender L J.Hooker.*

OPPOSITE: *Although sails, ropes and timber seem far removed from the electronic and metallic world of the modern navy, many navies around the world still use old sailing ships as training vessels. This beautiful three-master, a training vessel for the Russian navy, was already surrounded by an escort of small craft, including the Sydney–Hobart yacht* Brindabella, *even though it was still nearly 20 km away from the Sydney heads.*

ABOVE: *It is Boxing Day and the start of the Sydney to Hobart yacht race. Thousands of people, like brightly coloured ants, clamber around the rocky promontory which is the harbour's North Head, all trying to find the best vantage point to watch the ocean-going racers, spinnakers up and sails set, head out through the Heads.*

OPPOSITE: *The Manly Ferry* Narrabeen *battles her way through a heavy swell on the half-hour voyage to Circular Quay from Manly.*

OVERLEAF: *An unusual start with sails and spinnakers set against a darkening summer sky, competitors in the 1994 Sydney to Hobart yacht race speed through the harbour heads. Once at sea, they turn south and battle their way down the coast of New South Wales and Victoria before crossing Bass Strait and heading for the finishing line in Hobart.*

ABOVE: *An Australian Oberon Class submarine, crew at the ready and preparing to berth in Sydney Harbour, cuts through the waters of the Pacific outside the Heads.*

ABOVE: *One of the most delightful products of the worldwide movement to protect whales has been their increasing presence along the Sydney coastline. They make their way north in May–June to their breeding grounds off the coast of Queensland and return, often with their new calves, between September and November. In recent times, mothers and calves have stayed along the coast for days and have even entered Sydney harbour. This whale was photographed off Curl Curl, a popular northern surfing beach near Manly.*

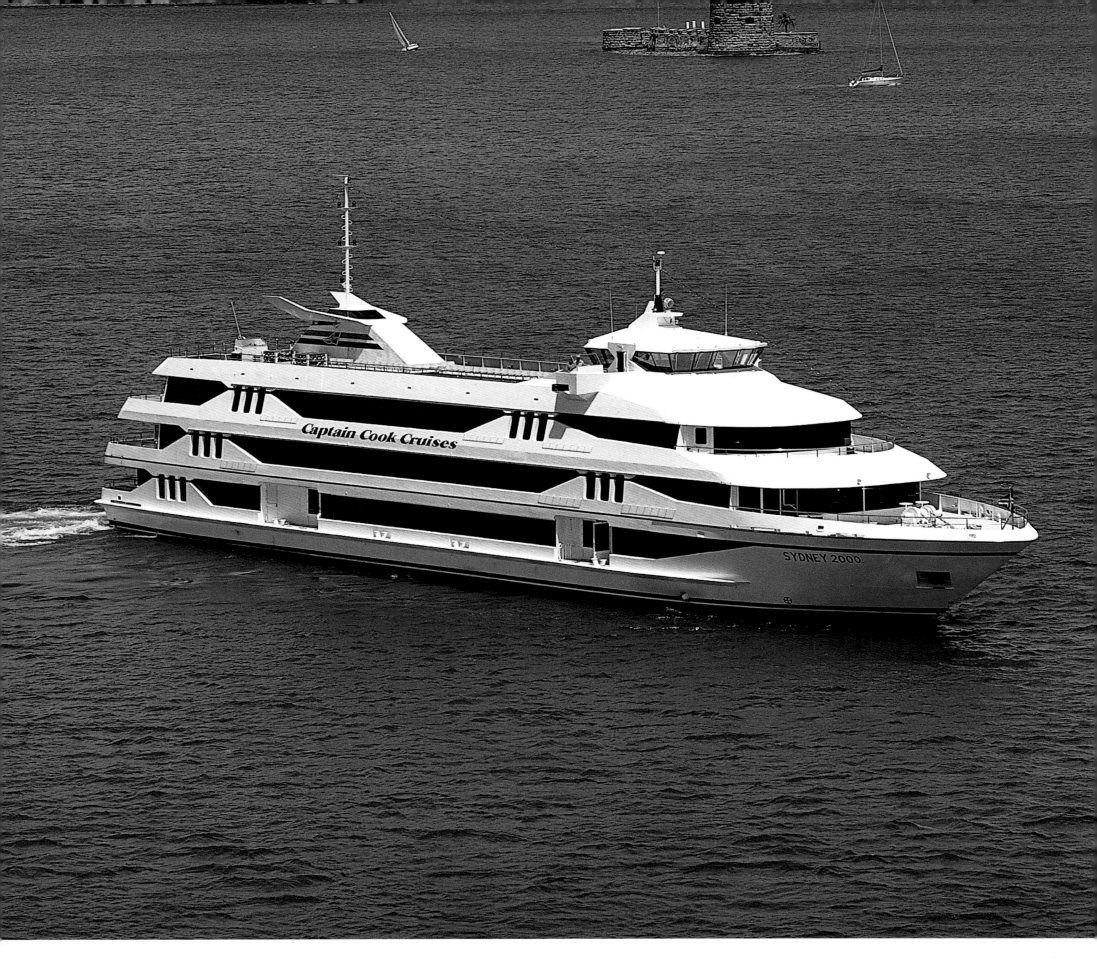

One of Sydney's most popular day trips is a voyage around
the harbour foreshores with Captain Cook Cruises. Here the
company's modern cruise vessel crosses the harbour to the
north of Fort Denison.

There was a time when travel across Sydney Harbour was a leisurely activity. Ferries plied the waters from Circular Quay to a variety of northern wharves which stretched from Manly to the inner reaches of the Parramatta River. In recent times, many of these ferries have been replaced by high powered vessels like this River Cat, which takes passengers from Circular Quay to Parramatta. For harbour lovers who rejoiced in the languid journeys, these new speedsters, which scud across the surface of the harbour, are viewed with admiration tinged with sadness.

OPPOSITE: *Into a misty, early morning harbour dark, with threatening rainclouds and edging into an overcast day, glides one of the world's great ocean liners, the* Crystal Symphony. *It will moor near the city centre.*
ABOVE: *Moored in the harbour waiting to berth, the*

Norwegian Star *gets special free entertainment as the annual Sydney Harbour ferry race, surrounded by hundreds of pleasure craft, comes scudding up the harbour.*

OVERLEAF: *In recent years, Sydneysiders have decided that*

Australia Day, celebrated on 26 January, the day Captain Arthur Phillip sailed into Sydney Cove, is a cause for a party. Apart from the fireworks display at night, during the course of the day, the harbour is covered with pleasure craft, yachts, cruisers, ferries and even the occasional sailing ship.

OPPOSITE: *A view of the famous King's Cross, which apart from its reputation within Australia is probably known well by servicemen from all over the world who have at some time in their lives found themselves on leave in Sydney. While 'the Cross' may be seedier these days than it once was, it has never lost the glamour of its colourful past. In the early part of the twentieth century, it was home to artists and writers, gradually becoming popular with the more bohemian among the population. Mid-century, came the brothels and illegal gaming houses, while the illegal drug industry, which flourishes in every western city, developed in the sixties and seventies. Whatever, 'the Cross' is still 'the Cross', and is worth a visit.*

RIGHT: *Each year, tens of thousands of Sydneysiders (and some very serious runners from around the world) line up in the city centre and run out through the eastern suburbs to Bondi Beach. It is the famous 'City to Surf' and, while it is supposed to be a fun run (hundreds of people get dressed up and do eccentric things), there is a definite competitive edge to it, with the great runners being sorted from the weekend enthusiasts on the infamous 'Heartbreak Hill' beyond Rose Bay.*

121

RIGHT: *At Randwick Racecourse, the punters are out and the air is full of the excitement of a day at the races on Derby Day, 29 April 2000.*

It is not really a Sydney game. AFL, Australian Rules as it is commonly known, or 'aerial pingpong' as its detractors insist on calling it, is a game played in Victoria, South Australia, Western Australia, Tasmania and the Northern Territory. Still, with the arrival of a local team, the Sydney Swans, the game's popularity has grown dramatically. It is now common for the Sydney Cricket Ground to be packed with enthusiastic supporters.

In the beginning, Sydneysiders knew it as 'the Showground'. Every year farmers from all over New South Wales would bring their produce and livestock to the Showground at Easter time and tens of thousands of people would visit the Royal Easter Show. Times change. The Royal Easter Show is now held near the Olympics site and the Showground and all its ancillary buildings has been renamed Fox Studios. It is here that stars like Tom Cruise and Nicole Kidman work and movies like the Oscar-winning 'The Matrix' are made. There are also restaurants, a multiplex cinema and a movie theme park.

PREVIOUS PAGES: *Beyond Kings Cross, the harbour shoreline is simply headland and bay, headland and bay. Here, from above Point Piper, and looking east towards the Pacific Ocean, the eye moves across Elizabeth Bay and past Elizabeth Point to Rushcutters Bay.*

RIGHT: *It has been said that you need at least $1 million to have a residence with a view of Sydney Harbour. That figure can be multiplied many times if you want a waterfront residence on Darling Point. Located only 4 km from the city centre and boasting views up and down the harbour, Darling Point (named after the wife of Governor Ralph Darling) has been known as a suburb for the rich since the nineteenth century, when the residents included the innovative meat exporter, Thomas Mort; the department store owner, Samuel Hordern; the Tooth and Reschs families, both famous brewers; and Reverend George Macarthur, rector of the beautiful St Marks Anglican Church and headmaster of The Kings School. Among the elegant buildings on the foreshore is Lindesay, the first mansion built on Darling Point and now owned by the National Trust in New South Wales.*

OVERLEAF: *This photograph shows from the left, Double Bay, Point Piper, Woollahra Point, Rose Bay, Vaucluse and finishes with Steel Point and Neilson Park on the right. For many years, Rose Bay was famous for its flying boat base, and flying boats took off from here to islands off the coast and to destinations up and down the coast. Today, numerous flying boats weave their way with amazing accuracy between the pleasure craft and the marinas which crowd this attractive and popular eastern suburbs seaside recreation area.*

LEFT: *The neat patchwork of roofs that is Paddington in Sydney's eastern suburbs is a result of a building boom which occurred in the new suburb between 1860 and 1890. The attractive buildings are renowned for their unique iron lacework balconies. The developers of the time put up rows of neat terraces that have become symbols of chic inner-city living today. Paddington is only 3 km from the centre of the city and Oxford Street, its main artery, is a fashionable street of clothing shops, booksellers, cafes and restaurants.*

OPPOSITE: *Over the years, Double Bay, noted for its excellent clothing shops and its European-style cafes, has developed a reputation as one of Sydney's most sophisticated and urbane suburbs. In this view, Double Bay is seen over Darling Point.*

LEFT: *Between South Head and the city lie the charming inlets of Watsons Bay (home of the city's famous Doyles Restaurant), Parsley Bay and Vaucluse Bay. This is one of the city's wealthiest harbourside locations. Fortunately, large tracts—notably Neilsen Park and the lands around historic Vaucluse House—have been saved for the enjoyment of all Sydneysiders. This view shows Vaucluse Point in the top left, followed by Vaucluse Bay, Parsely Bay, Village Point, Watsons Bay, Laings Point, Camp Cove, Lady Jane Beach, South Head and around to the Gap.*

ABOVE: *When the sailing ship* Dunbar *mistook The Gap for Sydney Heads and was wrecked with the loss of 120 lives, it was decided to build Hornby Light on the tip of South Head. As early as 1790, a signal station was established there to indicate the location of the new settlement to ships which did not realise that the colony had moved from Botany Bay to Sydney Harbour. In 1818, the convict architect Francis*

Greenway completed the Macquarie Light, which remained until the present light was completed in 1883. It stands tall, white and gracious at the top of the hill above The Gap, with the city and the harbour behind it.

OPPOSITE: *It might sound intimidating in a city famous for its sharks to go swimming at Shark Beach in Shark Bay, but in*

summertime thousands of Sydneysiders flock to the protected Shark Beach in Neilsen Park, a delightful retreat characterised by extensive lawns and fine stands of cool trees. It is an ideal location for a summer picnic and the perfect family day out.

OPPOSITE AND RIGHT: *There is no better way to see the city than by air. In the soft afternoon light, as the bridge casts a long shadow across the harbour, a small single-wing aeroplane banks and swoops over the harbour. A replica of the famous British biplane, the Vickers Vimy, flies across Sydney Cove. It is no accident that it is registered as G-EAOU. It's an optimistic cry for help from people in a very old plane and stands for 'God 'Elp All Of Us. The original aircraft was the one in which Sir Ross and Sir Keith Smith first flew from England to Australia in 1919.*

PAGE 140: *The Royal Australian Air Force acrobatic aerial team, the Roulettes, go through their paces above Sydney Harbour. It is not everyday that one can see them from above.*

PAGE 141: *The famous supersonic aeroplane, the Concorde, occasionally comes to Australia. This recent picture of the Air France aircraft was taken above Sydney Airport.*

Helicopters at play. As with the photo on page 10, this amazing photograph was taken when the Aerospeciale Tigre was being put through its paces over Sydney.

OPPOSITE: *The gracious buildings, elegant parklands and playing fields of St Ignatius College (one of the city's premier Jesuit schools) stand on a headland at Riverview. Overlooking the waters of the harbour, the views stretch across to the harbour bridge and the city centre.*

RIGHT: *Sydney's Taronga Zoo can boast some of the best views in the world. It was opened in 1916 and on 24 September that year the first ferry from Circular Quay to the zoo carried an elephant named Jessie. A regular passenger ferry service was established soon after. Voted the best international zoo in 1992, Taronga Zoo has both superb views over Sydney Harbour and a substantial collection of Australian native fauna.*

145

Another of those gems of beauty and valued real estate is the area where Middle Harbour meanders inland from the main Sydney Harbour. Known as The Spit, the tranquil waters are ideal for mooring marine craft of all kinds and the views from every angle are breathtaking. The bridge spans a narrow neck of water at the end of what was once a long spit of sand jutting across the bay to the steeper slopes below what is now Seaforth. The bridge is an opening bridge and restricts tall marine craft to specific times for navigation further up Middle Harbour. The bridge forms part of the main motor traffic route to the city from Manly and the communities to the north.

OVERLEAF: *Surrounded by tugboats gently nudging her to her berth, the mighty QE2 arrives in Sydney Cove. She will berth on the western side of Circular Quay, a perfect resting place where passengers will gaze across at the Opera House.*

PREVIOUS PAGES: *The size of Sydney's central business district was constrained by the harbour until the late 1960s when, in a brief and dramatic leap, it crossed the harbour and the office blocks of North Sydney appeared. Today, North Sydney, an important business centre and the home of advertising agencies, computer, communication and high tech companies. is edged by the Warringah Expressway (which offers access to both the bridge and the harbour tunnel). At the northern end of the office development, North Sydney Oval—a cricket and football sportsground—is a reminder of the suburb's more leisurely recent past.*

LEFT: *A ridge rises from Milsons Point at the northern side of the Harbour Bridge all the way to Hornsby, the city's northernmost suburban centre. Along this ridge run the Pacific Highway and the railway line. At various vantage points, the ridge affords exceptional views over the city. At North Sydney, those who occupy one of the upper floors in the suburb's new highrise buildings can see across the harbour and all the way to the heads.*

153

RIGHT: *The modern city of Parramatta was once the seat of Government in the new colony of New South Wales. The rich soil and plentiful fresh water made it ideal as a settlement and by the 1790s it had become quite a large town. Old Government House which can be found in Parramatta Park today is the oldest vice-regal residence in Australia and was first built by Governor Phillip in 1790. Rebuilt by Governor Hunter in 1799 and improved during Governor Macquarie's time, Old Government House was the preferred home of colonial governors until the 1850s. Parramatta has always played an important part in Sydney's development and has seen continual growth since its beginnings. Between 1950 and 1990, the centre of Sydney moved 23 km west from the CBD to Parramatta, which is now the hub of the city's Greater West. It is the economic power-house of the city, and thus of the entire country.*

LEFT: *One of Sydney's premier attractions for children and young adults is Australia's Wonderland, set in the heart of the city's vast greater western suburbs. It is the country's largest theme park and includes a Hanna Barbera Land, a Goldrush area which includes a huge wooden roller coaster and a 'Snowy River Rampage' whitewater adventure, Transylvania—with a Demon rollercoaster which twists 360°, a wildlife park, an artificial beach and an open-air theatre which offers a variety of entertainment.*

OPPOSITE: *Alhough the Sydney Olympics 2000 will be concentrated at Homebush Bay, the entire city will be utilised. There will be events at Penrith, Ryde, Blacktown, Bondi, Darling Harbour and a number of other venues. A special rowing venue has been constructed at Penrith, the city's traditional home of rowing and the site of the famous private school rowing competition, the Head of the River.*

To the west of the city, on the edge of the Blue Mountains, lies the Warragamba Dam, the city's primary fresh water supply. The completion of the Warragamba Dam in the late 1950s flooded the Burragorang Valley and the residents were moved to neighbouring towns. The dam was built to supply the growing population of Sydney, which had experienced acute water shortages during the drought of the 1930s. Warragamba Dam is said to be the largest dam in the Southern Hemisphere. The lake created by the waters covers 7500 hectares.

OPPOSITE: *Since the railway arrived in the late nineteenth century, the Blue Mountains to the west of Sydney have been a popular holiday destination where people wanting to escape the humidity of the city's summer months could enjoy a cool and embracing climate as well as spectacular scenery. One of the newest hotels is Peppers Fairmont at Leura, which is located beside the Leura Golf Course and offers visitors splendid views across the Jamieson Valley to the sheer cliffs of the area's impassible box canyons.*

RIGHT: *Katoomba is recognised as the main centre in the Blue Mountains. It is where the tourist buses stop and where visitors can cross the Jamieson Valley on the Scenic Skyway, drop 230 metres into the valley on the Scenic Railway and, at Echo Point on the edge of the valley, enjoy exceptional views of the Three Sisters (OVERLEAF), Mount Solitary and the Ruined Castle.*

PAGES 164 AND 165: *In past years, the Central Coast, the area to the north of Sydney, was a dormitary to Sydney. It is now a vibrant centre with its own industry. This view shows Umina, Woy Woy and the Brisbane Waters reaching across to Gosford.*

PAGES 166 AND 167: *Victoria Road winds its way from the northwest into the city centre across Gladesville Bridge. With the bridge and the CBD in the background, this view from Gladesville gives a clear image of the drowned river valley that is now a wonderland of bays and inlets, every one dotted with yachts and cruisers. There are 13 islands in Sydney Harbour. Six are named after people and, of the others, there is a Goat Island, Shark Island, Snapper Island and Cockatoo Island. Shark Island wasn't named because of the sharks in the harbour, but because it has the shape of a shark. Goat Island, seen here, is now part of the Sydney Harbour National Park.*

RIGHT: *Going away or returning home, the airport is the starting point. This telephoto lens picture, while an exaggeration of optics, shows how close Sydney is to its International Airport.*

OVERLEAF: *When it was built in 1932, the Sydney Harbour Bridge was the largest steel arch bridge in the world, and 52 800 tonnes of steel were used in its construction. Today, it still stands as the centre and focal point of Sydney, carrying traffic 132 metres above sea level. Although there is now a tunnel under the harbour, the bridge is still the symbolic artery between the city's northern and southern suburbs.*

PAGES 172 AND 173: *Nestled underneath its huge arch of the Sydney Harbour Bridge is Luna Park which, as every Sydneysider knows, is 'just for fun'.*

RIGHT: *And so we bid farewell to Sydney. Having flown in, flown around the harbour, marvelled at the beauties and attractions of this remarkable harbour city, we fly away. As we cross over the harbour bridge, groups of climbers (now one of the city's most popular tourist activities) on the very top of the bridge's soaring arc wave us a friendly farewell.*

OVERLEAF: *When the English novelist Anthony Trollope visited Australia in 1873, he wrote of Sydney: 'I despair of being able to convey to any reader my own idea of the beauty of Sydney Harbour. I have seen nothing to equal it in the way of land-locked sea scenery.' How much more would he have despaired if he had been able to rise above the city and marvel at its beauty from the air?*

BACK ENDPAPER: *The arc of the world, the glorious and gentle circumference of this blue sphere we all live on, is captured perfectly from above the city with the magic of the Pentax fish-eye lens and the courage of Ron Israel who, at the moment of this exposure, was dangling out of the helicopter at a height of 12 000 feet (4000 metres) ensuring that neither the aircraft nor its occupants accidentally became part of this remarkable image.*

Index

SIGNED PRINT OFFER

If you've enjoyed looking at these wonderful aerial photographs and you'd like to own a frameable print of any of the images in this book, simply send your request to the publishers. We'll send you a digital print of the highest quality, personally signed by Ron Israel, which you'll be delighted to have on the walls of your home. The print sizes are 450 mm wide x 320 mm deep (image area 432 mm x 308 mm deep) for most photographs and 450 mm wide x 164 mm deep (image area 432 mm wide x 157 mm deep) for photographs taken with the panoramic camera. The price for each print is $150.00 (no quantity discounts) including GST, packing and postage anywhere in Australia.

Simply send your order to Murray David Publishing Pty Ltd, 35 Borgnis Street Davidson, NSW, 2085. Please include your name, address, phone number and other contact details, along with your cheque or other payment details and the page number of the photograph you want. You can fax your order to (02) 9451 3663 or email to murraydavid@bigpond. com. Please allow 30 days for delivery as prints will be produced to order. You can pay by cheque, money order or by Mastercard, Bankcard or Visa (don't forget to sign and give full credit card details including card expiry date).

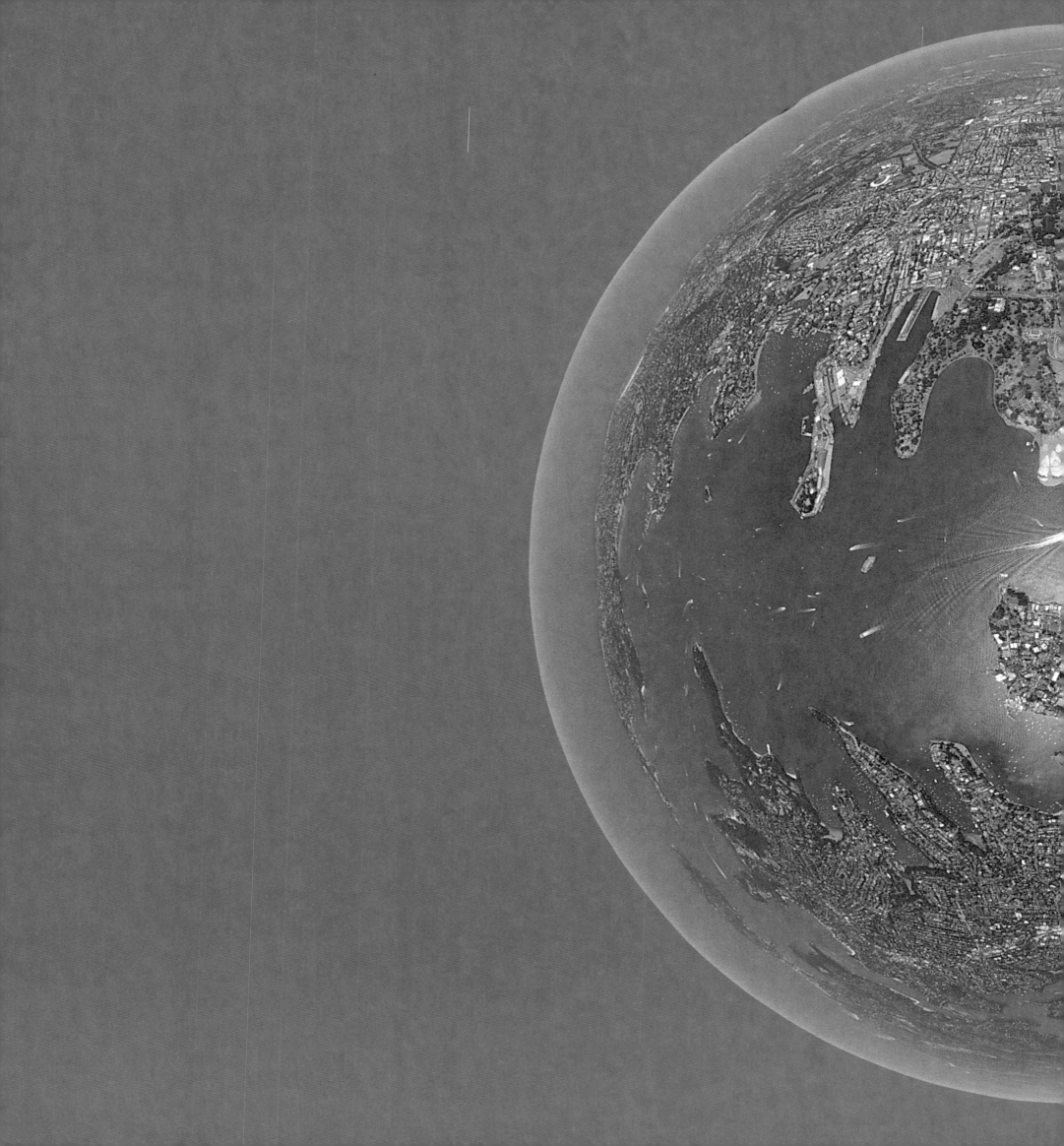